PACEY LOSES A TOOTH

Written by Dr. Paul Williams

ISBN 978-1-7361357-6-1 paperback

Published by Pirend

www.pirend.com

Pacey Loses A Tooth

Sunshine bright, a day so fine,
Pacey and friends, all in a line.
They jump, laugh and swing up high,
So happy, underneath the clear, blue sky.

Jump rope twirling, Pacey's turn is near,
His friends chant his name, faces full of cheer.
One, two, three, he jumps with might,
But then, oh dear, something isn't right.

The rope catches his feet, and he stumbles and falls,
The world seems to spin, as the playground stalls.
Pacey doesn't cry out, nor shed a single tear,
But he feels something's amiss, something quite clear.

Pacey holds his mouth, a surprise in store,
One of his teeth doesn't feel like before.
Now fear has Pacey firmly gripped,
As he knows his tooth is badly chipped.

Off to his mom, he runs with a bound,
Hoping she'll know why his tooth feels so round.
"Oh dear!" Momma Potto exclaims, seeing the sight,
"Your tooth is broken, it's not quite right!"

So, they're off with a quick skip and a dash,
They go to straight to Dr. Dennis, in a flash.
As they enter the clinic, Pacey looks around,
There are kids with bright smiles, not a single frown.

Dr. Dennis' place is filled with delight,
With toys and books, and colors so bright.
A fish tank bubbles, with fish swimming free,
It's such a happy place, as clear as can be.

"Don't worry, young Pacey," Dr. Dennis appears in the aisle,
"I will restore your beautiful and happy smile."
"Do you know about the Tooth Fairy, so crafty and neat?
"She leaves presents for kids, making their day so sweet!"

A present for me? Pacey thinks with glee,
For a tiny lost tooth? Oh, what could it be?
He imagines toys, candies, and even a kite,
Every possibility fills his heart with delight.

"But first," Dr. Dennis says, "let's take a good look,
With my special tooth camera, and this little book."
Pacey opens his mouth, as wide as can be,
And Dr. Dennis examines him, very carefully.

"I see the problem," Dr. Dennis sounds so sure,
"Don't you worry, I'll fix your teeth, just like they were.
Now, let's prepare the tooth, give it some rest,
With some sleepy juice, that's the best!"

The juice takes effect, the tooth starts to doze,
And Pacey feels funny, from his head to his toes.
The doctor says, "now lie back, and hold this near,
It's a special pillow, to keep your tooth clear."

As Pacey lies back, he thinks of his day,
Of jump ropes and games, of lively play.
He remembers the fall, the shock and the fright,
And hopes the friendly Tooth Fairy will come tonight.

Pacey's teeth rest on the pillow, feeling so snug,
Dreaming of tooth fairies, waiting for a hug.
Then comes Mr. Pusher, so strong and neat,
Making sure Pacey's tooth is fast off its feet.

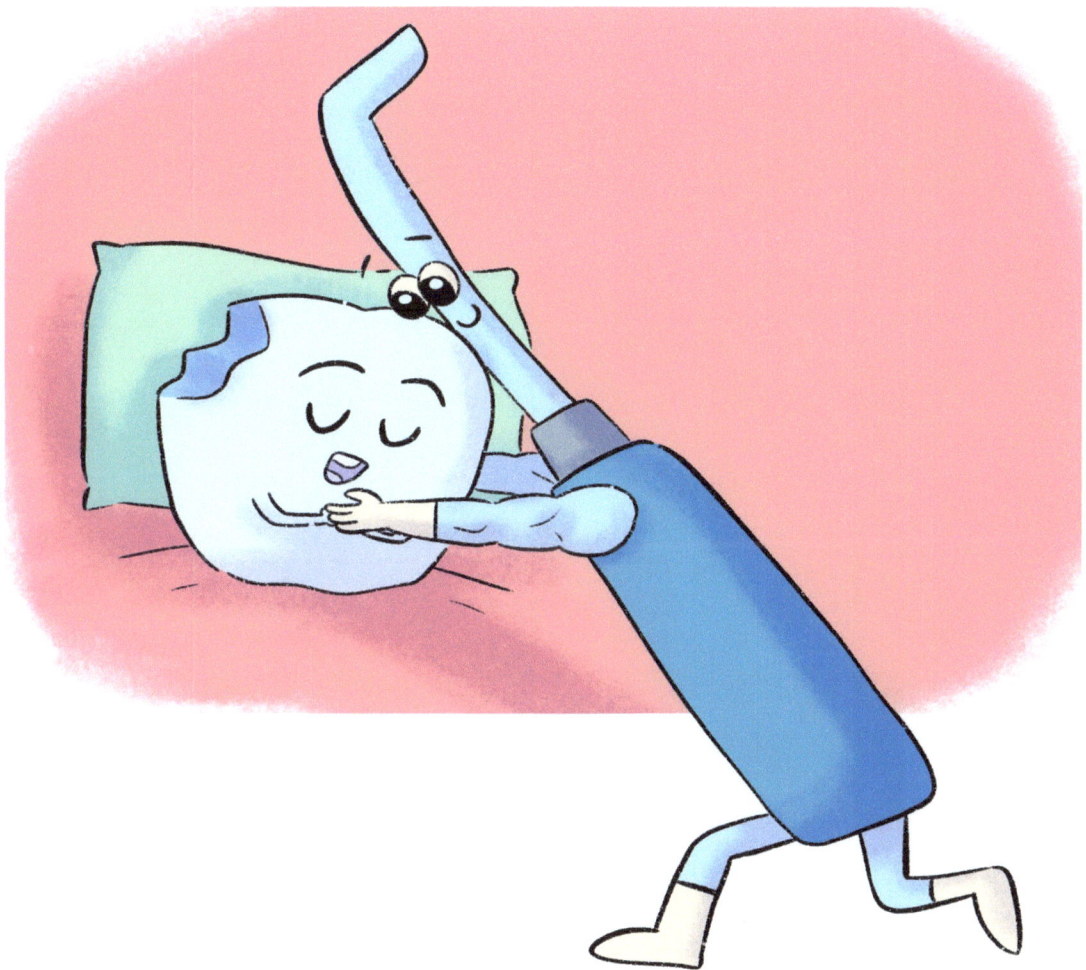

With a gentle push here and a nudge there,
Mr. Pusher works with such gentle care.
Next comes the Tooth Hugger, so soft and so kind,
He takes the sleepy tooth, leaving no trace behind.

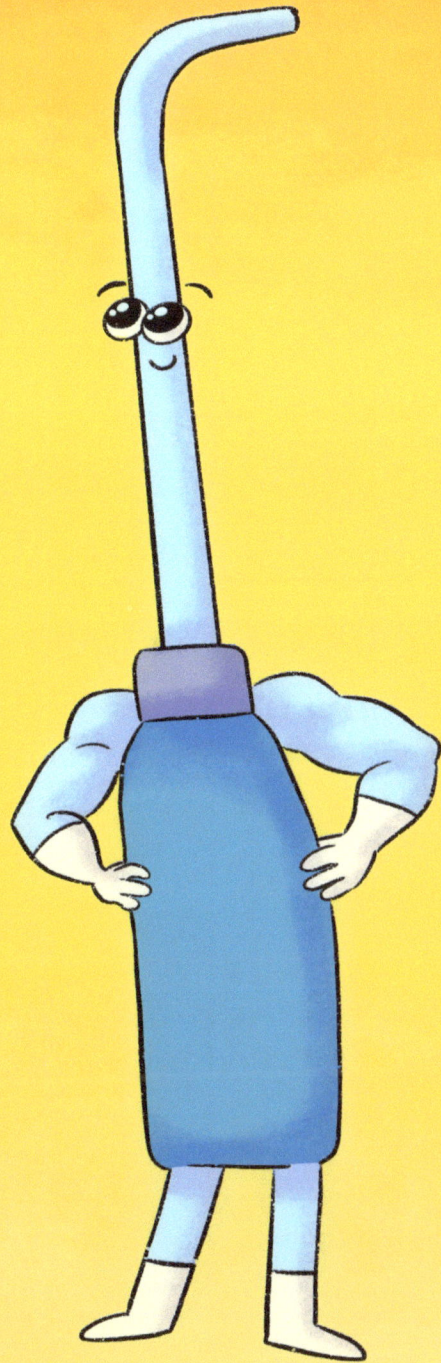

With the procedure over, Pacey's all done,
He gets his tooth wrapped up, oh what fun!
Pacey's gap-toothed smile lights up his face,
Knowing a new tooth will soon take its place.

"Now I'll get a present!" Pacey exclaims with delight,
Ready for the Tooth Fairy to come, later that night.
Under his pillow, the tooth present goes,
Pacey wonders what he'll get. Nobody knows.

He dreams of treasures, as he drifts into the night,
Hoping the Tooth Fairy would soon take flight.
As the moon shines bright, a silhouette appears,
Spreading her fairy dust and gleeful cheers.

She takes Pacey's tooth, leaving a gift so neat,
Morning would reveal, the surprise so sweet.
Dawn breaks and Pacey wakes. "I can't wait to see,
"What the generous Tooth Fairy left for me!"

But we won't spoil the surprise, oh no, not today,
What did the Tooth Fairy give Pacey? What do you say?
Could it be a toy, a book, or shiny new drums?
What will you wish for, when your turn comes?

Every lost tooth will bring something new,
What would the Tooth Fairy bring for you?

9 781736 135761